FINALLY: THE GOLF SWING'S

SIMPLE SECRET

A revolutionary method proved for the weekend golfer to significantly improve distance and accuracy from day one

"Every weekend golfer should read this great book" - Camilo Villegas

J. F. TAMAYO • 143 Photographs by J. Jaeckel

"To my kids, María, Juan Felipe and Santiago. Hopefully this work will help them develop the love for the game that will make their lives more enjoyable." – J.F. TAMAYO

FINALLY: THE GOLF SWING'S SIMPLE SECRET
COPYRIGHT © 2010 JUAN F TAMAYO

FIRST EDITION

ISBN: 1449596924
EAN-13: 9781449596927

CONTENTS

🙂 Correct

🙁 Incorrect

1. BACKGROUND

I was born in Colombia, a small country where golf is a very exclusive game and not a popular sport. Just to give you an idea, today there are approximately 20,000 golfers in Colombia versus more than 30 million in the United States of America. Thanks to our star, Camilo Villegas, we now have a live broadcast of the PGA Tour tournaments on TV every week and golf has increased in interest and popularity.

I was fortunate enough to start to play golf when I was a kid. My friends and I rapidly developed a passion for the game and we had the opportunity to play a lot, practice a lot and compete amongst us. Still, neither of us ever got a chance to play real good golf. For many years we were all blocked in the upper single digit handicap range, which I believe is very mediocre for anyone who gets the chance to start to play at such a short age.

Although my interest, dedication and passion for golf never changed, my golf level did not improve for many years, making this process a very frustrating one. I clearly remember the times when I was hitting the ball pretty well and shot a great round of golf, which made me believe I had finally learned how to play. Unfortunately this short illusion was always diluted by the next terrible round of golf, where suddenly I felt I had totally lost my swing and I had no idea on how to fix it.

The reason for not improving was very simple. We all grew up with very limited knowledge of the fundamentals and essentials of the golf swing. Our golf teachers were people who became good players and taught us the golf swing theory in terms of their understanding and personal experience. We learned how to play golf in a very intuitive way.

It was only until my college years when I had a chance to read David Leadbetter's book "The Golf Swing", that I understood two basic rules:

1. The fundamentals and essentials of the golf swing had already been invented and

2. The only sustainable way to improve and to hit consistently solid golf shots was to develop and implement a consistently solid golf swing.

Today, 15 years later, I am very confident to say that since then I have read the most important golf instructional books written so far. I have read and studied in detail David Leadbetter's "Lessons from the Golf Greats", "Positive Practice" and "Faults and Fixes", Butch Harmon's "The four Cornerstones of Winning Golf", Faldo's "Play like the Pro's", Stan Utley's "The art of Putting/Chipping" and "The art of Scoring", Tiger Wood's "How I play Golf", Phil Mickelson's "Secrets of the Short Game", Dave Peltz's "Putt like the Pros", all Bob Rotella´s mental books including his latest and outstanding "Your 15th Club", Jim Hardy's "The Plane Truth for Golfers", Ralph Mann's "Swing like the Pro's", "Ben Hogan's Five Lessons: The Modern Fundamentals of Golf", Hank Haney's "The Essentials of the Golf Swing" and Jim Mclean's recent release "The Slot Swing", just to mention a few.

I also film my swing regularly to analyze it and compare it versus the swings of the best players in the world using "Leadbetter Interactive" computer software. Additionally, I enjoy to watch high definition slow motion tour player's swings through the Swingplex application of the PGA Tour and the swings recorded with the Konica Minolta Swing Vision camera that are usually available from www.youtube.com.

It is important to notice that I have never been interested in becoming a professional golfer. I am the manager of a corporation that provides a loyalty program in Colombia for Carrefour, the second largest supermarket in the world and I only get to play golf at the most once a week. The only reason for me to have studied and learned is because golf is my hobby, my sport and my passion. As I am also a weekend golfer and I have your same time restrictions, this book has been written from your same point of view. I truly understand your limitations and obstacles for becoming a better player. Still, today, I am very happy to share with you the incredible break-through that I made throughout these years which can make the golf swing so much easier to learn, to perform and to repeat.

The interesting contribution that I expect to make to golf instruction is to offer the weekend golfer the first real, fast, easy and effective method that will significantly improve his consistency, distance and ball striking. Throughout these years of understanding how difficult and complex the golf swing can become, I have been able to develop and create a revolutionary method I truly believe would help you learn how to develop, repeat and maintain, throughout the years, a solidly sound golf swing.

You won't need to spend long hours on the practice range. All that I teach can be learned and practiced at your home or office in front of a mirror and most of the time without a golf club. Once you master my technique, you can easily take it to the golf course and do exactly the same. Just at this time, you will apply my method with a golf club in your hands. It is as simple as that.

This book is dedicated to ordinary people, like me, who either can only play once a week or who have been struggling for a long time to get better. You don't need to be an Olympic athlete nor have any special physical ability. Everyone who follows my method will improve dramatically. It is only a matter of understanding and rehearsing a few but major changes that will make your swing be more structured and looking more like the best players' swings. I know with precision what needs to be thought and done to make a swing look more like the pros plus I am convinced anyone who is really interested in trying is capable of making these changes.

To be more specific, this book is dedicated to the following type of players:

1.   THE WEEKEND GOLFER who cannot wait until it is Saturday to play, enjoys sharing 18 holes with his friends and would love to improve, but doesn't have the time to practice, nor the interest to learn the mechanical details of the golf swing. To get an idea, this player may often take a golf lesson but will never be interested in filming his swing for further analysis. His level of game has been the same for the last couple of years.

2.   THE STRUGGLING GOLFER who is really interested in taking his game to a higher level but has not been able to do so, at least at the pace that he was expecting. He reads golf books and magazines, tries different theories and tips and has more time to practice, but he is not improving at the rate he wishes or deserves.

If you belong to any of these groups, I really believe I have something new that could help your game immediately. My point of view as a weekend golfer, as you, can make me imagine how difficult it has been for you to make any changes in your golf swing and how often these changes didn't work.

So my sincere invitation is to give yourself one last chance and try my system. Give me the opportunity to show you that you are more than capable of taking your golf game to the next level.

Believe me, it can be done in a short period of time. Don't be afraid of implementing the changes I will ask you to perform and pretty soon you will be surprising your golf partners.

So let's begin....

2. INTRODUCTION

Have you ever wondered why the average handicap on the USGA has barely improved in the last 20 years at the same time when 1) technology and equipment innovations have surpassed levels anyone could have ever imagined and 2) access to knowledge of the golf swing has broaden since there has been a proliferation of books and articles written by the best teachers, coaches and players worldwide?

No one can argue that new technologies in the construction of golf balls and clubs have made it possible for anyone to hit longer and straighter balls, even on miss-hit shots. Inventions like the titanium drivers have helped all skilled players, including tour players, to increase the average driver distance from 257 yards in 1980 to 288 yards in 2009, according to statistics published at www.pgatour.com. So, although it would be hard to conclude, I truly believe that this gain in distance as well as the higher forgiveness offered in today's clubs is the only reason why the average USGA men's handicap has timidly dropped from 16 in 1990 to 14.5 in 2008 and women's USGA average handicap has only dropped from 30 to 27.5. (Reference: Article "The Shapes: Evolution of Improvement", Golf Digest Magazine, February 2009 by Mike Stachura).

The best teachers and coaches in the world such as David Leadbetter, Butch Harmon, Jim McLean, Dave Peltz and Hank Haney, just to mention a few, have done an outstanding job of understanding and sharing their incredible knowledge of the fundamentals and essentials of the golf swing through their books, videos, DVDs and academies.

So having the best technology and information available, the question remains unanswered: Why hasn't the average weekend golfer significantly improved over the last decade?

The answer is very simple:

a.   The Golf Swing is very difficult to understand and to perform, and specially the backswing where you need to simultaneously rotate your shoulders more than 90 degrees at a plane perpendicular to your spine angle, rotate your arms at a much more upright plane and hinge your wrists towards the sky, all this at the same time, in a very coordinated way, while resisting the lower body so it doesn't turn more than 45 degrees, thus, creating the coil and consistency necessary to generate power and accuracy. If this sounds complicated, I better not even mention the level of complexity of understanding and performing the flattening and change of plane of the shaft that takes place during the transition of the backswing and downswing that is needed to create lag and to hit solid shots on the traditional two plane golf swing.

b. The average weekend golfer would love to improve but doesn't have the time or the commitment to do so. The hard work and the long hours of practice required, many times with frustrating results, is something that the majority of players cannot afford or are not interested enough in doing so. Under the traditional methods, if someone really wants to improve, there is a pretty good chance he needs to make changes in his grip, posture, alignment, backswing, transition, downswing, follow-through and finish. And we all know that this would be an extremely difficult task to achieve. Plus, based on the experience of the majority of weekend players, including the ones that take lessons on a regular basis, they are aware that either there has been no improvement over the years or it has been much slower than expected. Some improve fast but suddenly get to a point where they get blocked and cannot get any better, no matter how much they read or any tip they try.

Having developed a revolutionary learning method with the easiest and fastest way to have a significant improvement in any golfer of any level who applies my system, my goal is to have the most read golf book as a consequence of a growing "word of mouth" that I expect through the years, as my readers happily share their positive experiences with other golfers when they see and feel their significant improvements obtained in a short period of time.

My method has been developed under three main principles:

1. FIRST PRINCIPLE: FOCUS ON CHANGES THAT MOST POSITIVELY AFFECT RESULTS: I would only ask a player to make changes in the most relevant parts of the swing needed to hit solid and consistent shots. Adding just a simple feature to their posture, this book will mainly focus on the backswing and on the transition between the backswing and the downswing. If any player of any level learns the backswing and transition that I will teach, he will definitely have a major improvement in his swing performance and in his ability to hit long, solid and consistent golf shots day after day. Of course a player that has a solid foundation of the grip, posture and alignment can rapidly expect to become a single digit handicapper while a higher handicapper with less sound foundations should lower his handicap very rapidly but should not expect a single digit in the near future. A high single digit, like I had been for 25 years before discovering and implementing this revolutionary method should expect to move to the lower single digit zone very fast. I have now been between a scratch and a 3 handicap player for the last couple of years after implementing my system, although I only play once a week and rarely have the time to practice my long game on the practice range.

About 30% of the breakthrough of my method is very simple. The traditional teaching system starts from the basics. The student will first need to fix his grip, posture, setup and alignment. Any of these changes, even if they are minor, would be extremely difficult and uncomfortable to achieve, and yet would only have a minor effect on the ball striking and distance performance, when compared to an improvement done on the backswing and transition. On the other hand, I believe that if you learn how to develop a solid backswing and transition with your accustomed grip, posture and setup, may not make you a scratch player overnight, but would definitely make you a much better player immediately. Still, you will have plenty of time in the future to fix these basic fundamentals (if needed) and continue to improve your ball flight and control, but only do it once you learn how to hit a ball more solidly.

2.   SECOND PRINCIPLE: LEARN HOW TO DEVELOP AN EASY, REPEATABLE AND YET SOUND AND SOLID BACKSWING: As I explained earlier, the orthodox and traditional two plane backswing is in my opinion too complicated and difficult, not only to understand but to perform properly and to repeat once you learn the theory. Also, the flattening of the shaft needed to bring the club back on plane on the downswing requires, not only great skill, but also amazing timing that is definitely not going to be there every time unless you practice 8 hours daily. On the other hand, there is a one plane swing, explained by Jim Hardy as a swing where "the arms swing upward onto somewhat the same plane the body turns". We can think of Ben Hogan as the classic example of a one plane swing. Even though I do believe this is an easier swing to learn, the chances that you would end up with a very flat backswing with too much rotation of the lower body that causes loss of power and consistency are high.

So, having studied the golf swing for several years, I was able to develop a unique and much easier way to consistently make a solid and sound backswing that will pretty much look like Tiger Wood's new one plane backswing but with two interesting characteristics:

a. It is much simpler to learn, to perform and to repeat as you only control and think of rotating and moving just one part of your body during the backswing. Take note that the rotation I would explain in detail later on is quite different from the rotation we have always been taught.

b. It is essentially solid and as long as you learn to rotate the way I would teach you, your backswing would look almost identical to many of the best players in the world. If you watch a slow motion backswing done when following this theory, you will notice that all the check-points of a perfect backswing would be achieved. The main difference is that this backswing is much simpler to learn, to perform and to repeat, requires less practice and is more reliable under pressure.

3. THIRD PRINCIPLE: LEARN HOW TO CREATE LAG: One of the most important aspects to achieve club speed and a pure ball strike, common in absolutely every tour player's golf swing, is "lag". Lag could be defined as the trailing of the club behind the hands during the downswing. If you ever heard of "Ben Hogan's magical move" it referred to this exact concept. The more lag you can create, the longer and better you will hit. This is why most teachers tell us to maintain the 90 degree angle formed by the left arm and the club during the backswing for as long as possible during the downswing (Picture 1 - pg 16). This proper motion, as opposed to coming over the top (Picture 2 - pg 16), will create lag thus generating an incredible acceleration of the clubhead through the impact zone.

 Picture 1. Backswing and downswing forming a 90 degree angle when left arm is parallel to the ground.

Picture 2. Incorrect downswing coming over the top.

Actually, the reason you see tour pros developing clubhead speeds many times above 125 MPH while doing an effortless and smooth swing has to do with the amount of lag they create. Not only do they maintain the 90 degree angle formed by the left arm and the club on the backswing during the downswing, but they also decrease this angle to 45 degrees or less, creating much more lag (distance between the clubhead and the hands), and thus achieving higher swing speeds, more distance and better ball striking (picture 3).

Later on I will explain in detail why lag creates higher clubhead speeds. Meanwhile, the good news I have to tell you today is that although it took me many years to understand how to create lag, once I learned the lesson, I can tell you, it is quite easy to repeat. Please take note that there is only one possible way to create lag and I will teach you exactly how to do so. Believe me that if you

Picture 3. Downswing increasing lag.

follow my instructions, you will be able to create the same amount the pro's do, even with a slower swing.

In summary, once you read this book you will discover and learn how to make an easier and more effective golf swing. My goal is to make you a better player without sacrificing valuable time you need for work or for family and friends. So good luck and my best wishes!

3. GOLF SWING´S FACTS AND RULES

The following are examples of some of the golf facts and rules that make the traditional learning method very difficult:

1. A typical golf lesson in a practice range looks as follows: The player arrives, hits a couple of bad shots and explains what is happening to his ball flight. Based on what the pro hears and sees, he suggests to the student to make some minor adjustments that can either be on the grip, posture, alignment, backswing, downswing or follow-through. The player immediately makes the changes and feels that he is hitting the ball much better until he plays his next round of golf where he finds that he didn't improve at all or that he shot a higher score than usual.

The interesting part of the story is that during the lesson the player felt he was making a dramatic change in his swing, but someone who may have been looking at his swing noticed no difference between the "before" and the "after" swings.

RULE #1: The only way to have a dramatic improvement in your ball hit, accuracy and distance is by having a dramatic improvement in the quality of your golf swing (Re-Engineering).

RULE #2: You may spend hours, days, weeks, months or years on the practice range hitting balls, but as long as you practice the same swing, you will always play the same golf.

RULE #3: The best and easiest way to improve a golf swing is to try to emulate a correct swing, instead of trying to fix a bad swing.

RULE #4: Once a player understands how to make a good swing, he will discover his new swing is much easier and more natural than the previous one that had many flaws.

2. Golf instruction books and videos are the best source of information regarding the fundamentals and essentials of the golf swing. Access to the lifetime knowledge and experience of the best players, teachers and coaches in the world has an incredible value. Still, the golf swing is so complicated, that this information will be specially useful to the most dedicated players who have the time and commitment to spend long hours on the practice range, who film and analyze their golf swings on a regular basis, and that have the time and patience to make changes in many parts of their swings. Also, note that the vast majority of golf instruction books start from the basics: grip, posture and alignment.

RULE #5: Most golf books have too much information and are very difficult to understand for the weekend golfer. For example, the only way to really understand what is the swing plane and how it behaves during the golf swing is to tape your swing.

RULE #6: A solid backswing and transition is the foundation of having great distance and solid ball striking. Working on these parts of the swing should be your first goal while trying to improve your swing. You will have plenty of time in the future to improve your grip, posture, and alignment once you learn how to hit a ball more solidly.

RULE #7: The only sustainable and effective method for the weekend golfer to understand and improve his swing is one that can be checked by himself in such a way that he would know if he is doing the correct swing without the need of cameras or more people.

3. All good players have a very coordinated backswing where they simultaneously rotate their shoulders and arms while hinging their wrists and resisting the lower body so it doesn't turn more than

45 degrees, creating the coil and consistency necessary to generate power and accuracy. During the transition of the backswing and downswing they flatten and change the plane of the shaft in order to create the lag necessary to hit solid shots. Most experts define "lag" as maintaining the 90° angle formed by the left arm and the club during the backswing for as long as possible during the downswing (picture 1 - pg 16). This master moves make their swings look very easy and smooth although they are creating club speeds over 125 MPH.

RULE #8: In golf, what you think is not what you get. It is extremely difficult, not to say impossible, to consciously control all movements simultaneously.

RULE #9: The key for a good swing is to turn properly and the majority of the weekend players don't understand how this rotation should be done.

RULE #10: The more lag that you can create, the longer and better that you will hit the golf ball. The best players in the world do not only maintain the 90 degrees angle formed by the left arm and the club during the backswing but they decrease this angle to 45 degrees during the downswing creating more lag, thus having higher swing speeds, more distance and better ball striking (picture 3 - pg 17).

4.   ONE PLANE vs TWO PLANE SWING

I decided to add this chapter just for reference purposes. You definitely do not need to read it or understand it to learn my method or to become a better player.

I only decided to include this comparison as I believe it could be more fun for you to watch golf tournaments on TV and to hear what commentators say when they analyze a golf swing, once you understand the main differences between the two most popular swings.

Next time you watch Peter Jacobsen, Michelle Wie, Chad Cambell, Steve Stricker, Zack Johnson, Ernie Els, Vijay Singh, Anthony Kim or Tiger Woods, for example, you will know they have a "one-plane" swing. On the other hand, once you see players like Sean O'hair,

David Toms, Davis Love III, Karrie Webb, Jim Furyk, Tom Watson or Retief Goosen you will rapidly know they are classic examples of a "two plane" golf swing.

Legends like Jack Nicklaus or Arnold Palmer had a "two-plane" swing while Sam Snead or Ben Hogan had a "one plane" swing.

Before I explain the golf swing plane, let me tell you that this is a concept that could only be understood by watching a golf swing from behind (down the line). Even if you already understand the swing plane theory, it would be extremely difficult for you to know your actual swing plane unless you tape your swing.

The swing plane is the angle or path at which the club, arms and shoulders travel around the body during a golf swing. The initial swing plane of any particular golf swing is determined by the angle formed by the shaft and the ground during the setup. The first observation that could be drawn is that this angle is different not only from player to player, but also for the same player depending on the club that he has in his hands. The longer the club is, for example a driver, the more shallow this angle would be as opposed to a shorter club like a Sand Wedge where the swing plane would begin in a much steeper angle as a consequence of being a shorter club (Pictures 4 and 5 - pg 29).

 Picture 4. Initial driver swing plane.   Picture 5. Initial sand-wedge swing plane.

In the "two -plane swing", this angle formed by the shaft changes dramatically during the golf swing as I will further explain it in a moment. On the other hand, on the pure "one plane swing", the angle stays intact during the golf swing. This is the case of Tiger Woods' swing where the club will always be on plane or parallel to the original plane. However, you will find many "one plane" swings where the club angle actually changes during the swing. Still, on these "one plane" swingers, the arms and shoulders would end up to be pretty much on the same angle on the top of the backswing.

So the main difference between these two golf swings is that on a "two plane" swing, the arms will turn in a much higher or steeper angle than the shoulders, while in the pure "one plane" swing the arms and the shoulders travel at pretty much the same angle. This is the reason why a "two plane" backswing would be more upright than a "one plane" backswing that would be more flat or baseball type.

So, based on the previous explanation, let me show you the main differences between the two swings. Please notice that I will only illustrate what happens during the backswing and during the transition since I don't want to lose focus on the essence of this golf book.

SETUP

Although this is not necessarily a rule, the main difference in a "two plane" swing is that the spine angle is more upright and doesn't bend as much as in the "one plane" swing. The reason is very simple. In both swings the shoulders usually turn perpendicular to the spine angle. However, as in the "one plane" swing the arms would swing up to be in the same angle of the shoulders at the top of the backswing, the player would end up with a very flat backswing unless he starts with a more bent spine. This is not a concern in a "two plane" swing as the arms would any way swing in a higher angle, thus ending up with a more upright backswing (Pictures 6 and 7).

 Picture 6. Typical setup and spine angle for a "two plane" swing.

Picture 7. Typical setup and more bent spine angle for a "one plane" swing.

BACKSWING – Midway

The point I like to check is in the middle of the backswing right where the left arm is parallel to the ground. At this point, a "two plane" swing has already started to turn the arms in a plane steeper than the shoulders. This is why you will notice that the shaft is now pointing somewhere in between the shoes and the golf ball (picture 8 - pg 32).

On the other hand, on the pure "one plane" swing, the shaft has never changed its angle and is still on plane or parallel to the original plane, thus pointing to the golf ball or even beyond (picture 9 - pg 32).

Picture 8. Halfway "two plane" backswing where arms turn in a steeper plane making shaft point between shoes and ball.

Picture 9. Perfect halfway "one plane" backswing with shaft on plane and pointing directly to the ball.

BACKSWING – Top

Here, the key for the "one plane" swing is to have the shoulders and the left arm exactly parallel to each other (picture 10). Depending on how long you make your backswing, it is very normal to have the club "laid-off" or pointing slightly to the left of the target. Meanwhile, on the "two plane" swing you will notice that the arms are now in a much higher angle than the shoulders resulting in a much more upright backswing (picture 11 - pg 34).

Picture 10. "One plane" backswing top with shoulders and left arm parallel to each other and club slightly laid-off.

Picture 11. "Two plane" more upright backswing top as arms are turned in a higher angle than the shoulders.

TRANSITION - DOWNSWING

Every good player starts the downswing from the feet up. This lower body action that initiates the transition between the backswing and the downswing is what creates lag and gets the swing in the correct plane (picture 12) to hit the ball solidly versus coming over the top (picture 13) as most amateurs do. Every good player, no matter if he has a one or a two-swing plane, comes back to the same "on-plane" position from the moment when the left arm gets parallel to the ground on the way down . Otherwise, when a player comes over the top, the shaft would appear to be much steeper at this stage.

In order to get to the correct position on the "two-plane" downswing, the player has to drop the hands and flatten the shaft. On the other hand, the "one-plane" swinger just starts to rotate and move the weight to the left to get to this optimal position, as the club was already on this plane or parallel to it. This is why you usually hear that it is much easier to be consistent with a "one-plane" swing. The plane change of the shaft that occurs on a "two-plane" swing makes this movement depend more on timing thus being more difficult to repeat consistently.

Picture 12. Both "one and two plane" downswings get to the correct plane when left arm is parallel to the ground.

Picture 13. Incorrect downswing coming over the top getting the shaft in a steeper plane.

5. MY METHOD: SETUP KEY

As I explained earlier, this book will focus only on the changes of your swing that will have the most benefit to your performance.

Of course the ideal golf swing will have a great grip, posture, setup and alignment as every tour player has. However, being able to make changes in these parts of the swing would be extremely difficult and uncomfortable to achieve and yet would only have a minor effect on the ball striking and distance performance, when compared to an improvement done on the backswing and transition. As I said before, you will have plenty of time in the future to fix these basic fundamentals (if needed) and continue to improve your ball flight and control, but you can work on these corrections once you learn how to hit a ball solidly.

There are only two key points in the setup that you must do in order to be able to achieve the backswing and transition that I want to teach you in the following chapters. In contrast to most changes in the grip, posture and alignment, the two changes that I need for you to make are very simple:

1.   FIRST SETUP CHANGE: SWING CONNECTION.
In the following chapter, I will teach you how to do a perfect backswing by only rotating or manipulating your shoulders properly. To be able to move the club, wrists and arms in a coordinated manner and in the correct path while only thinking of moving your shoulders, you must have your arms well connected to your body.

To create this connection, during the setup and before you begin your backswing, your upper arms must be touching and creating some pressure against the sides of your chest.

INSTRUCTIONS

1.   Take your normal stance as if you are going to hit a golf ball (picture 14).

2.   Move your Upper Arms towards your body so they touch and create pressure against the sides of your chest (picture 15).

Picture 14. Incorrect setup position with arms separated from the body.

Picture 15. Setup position with arms connected to the body.

CHECK-POINTS

1. Your arms should be straighter and closer to each other than they were before.

2. Your forearms might experience a slight twisting making your elbows be a little closer to each other and the inner side of the elbows point a little more towards the sky.

3. On a scale from 1 to 10, where 1 is the softest and 10 is the hardest, you should maintain a pressure of your arms on your chest of 4. In other words, you should definitely feel the connection but at the same time your arms and shoulders should be as relaxed as possible.

4. Half of your Upper Arms must be touching your chest. Therefore, the connection should begin from half of the distance from the elbows to the shoulders and up. If your entire Upper Arms touch your body it could be you're too close to the ball. On the other side, if less than half of your Upper Arms touch your body, either you are too far away from the ball or you are a little hunchbacked and you need to straighten your back.

2.   SECOND SETUP CHANGE: SOFT HANDS.

One of the big mistakes amateurs make is that they grab the club too hard. This is the kiss of death to good ball striking and distance. When you hold the club too tight, you don't hit the ball, you push the ball. You may swing the arms, but you do not let the club move or swing properly. As I will explain later on, one of the main keys for good ball striking and distance is being able to create lag. And believe me, it is impossible to create lag if you hold the club too tight. Imagine yourself throwing a tennis ball with your hand as far as you can. You would hold the ball very softly in your hand otherwise you would be unable to throw it very far.

INSTRUCTIONS

1.   Once you tighten your Upper arms towards your chest, you will do exactly the opposite with your hands. You will hold the club with your usual grip but as soft as you can.

CHECK-POINTS

1.   On a scale of 1 to 10, where 1 is the softest and 10 is the hardest, you want to hold the club maintaining a very light pressure of 3.

2.   You want to hold the club the softest you can without letting it slip from your hands. Since your grip is so soft, hypothetically someone could easily pull the club away from your hands and take it from you.

3.   You should feel that your hands and fingers are totally relaxed.

If you are at your home right now, you can try these changes in front of a mirror without a golf club. Although you will notice it is not difficult to incorporate them, you may feel it would be impossible to hit a ball like this.

It is absolutely normal for you to feel this way since probably you are accustomed to swing your arms and hands disconnected from your bigger muscles. You will feel it would be impossible to turn back having your arms close to your body. Actually, exactly the opposite is true. You may be right that it is impossible to swing the arms and hands back independently from your body with this posture, as most amateurs incorrectly do. However, this posture encourages you to turn your bigger muscles which are the keys for power instead of your smaller muscles like arms and hands that are usually the keys for inconsistency and lack of power.

Regarding how softly you are now holding the club versus how hard you held it your entire life will clearly explain why you feel it would be impossible to hit a ball this way. We incorrectly believe we need to control the entire swing making us want to hold the club too tight. At this point I can only ask you to believe me and soon you will be positively surprised when you start to strike the ball more solidly, getting a higher ball flight and hitting distances you had only dreamed about until now.

Please take note that **these two setup changes must be incorporated into your swing from day one and repeated on every long game golf shot you will hit in the future, with no exception**. The next two chapters, Backswing and Transition combined with this posture adjustment would make you improve dramatically. You do not have to implement the backswing and the transition theories simultaneously. Either one of the two, always combined with this new posture, should get you to play better golf in a short time. Of course, once you implement both your new backswing and transition you can expect a dramatic improvement in your golf game.

6. MY METHOD: BACKSWING

In my opinion, the most difficult part of the swing to understand and to learn is the backswing. In a good backswing you need to simultaneously rotate your shoulders more than 90 degrees at a plane perpendicular to your spine angle, rotate your arms at a much more upright plane and hinge your wrists towards the sky, all at the same time, in a very coordinated way and in the meantime resist the lower body so it doesn't turn more than 45 degrees. This creates the coil and the consistency necessary to generate power and accuracy.

Based on my observation, I can say than not more than 10% of the weekend golfers have a good backswing. It is extremely difficult, not to say impossible, to consciously control all these movements simultaneously. On the other hand, most of the few that do have a fairly good backswing have usually learned to play when they were young and they still struggle with it. They have to think of so many things to do properly that it is very common to see these players often get confused in their backswing. Suddenly, they don't know the correct path the club should take, they forget how to rotate their body, they get confused on what to think of their hands, arms and body in order to be able to start the swing, etc.

Still, a correct backswing is the foundation of a good swing. A good backswing is more than half of the equation needed to be able to hit the ball solidly, consistently and long. A good backswing will automatically improve your downswing even if you don't think about it. A good backswing will create the coil and the position necessary to hit the ball in the correct plane that will generate power and accuracy.

If you really want to have a dramatic improvement in your ball striking, accuracy and distance you must have a dramatic improvement in the quality of your backswing. You must understand that the best and easiest way to improve your backswing is to try to emulate a correct backswing, instead of trying to fix your actual one.

The great news is that you are about to learn a unique and much easier method to consistently make a solidly sound backswing.

You will rapidly discover that it is much simpler to learn, to do and to repeat as you only control and think of rotating just your shoulders during the backswing. As long as you learn to rotate your shoulders the way I will teach you, your backswing will look very similar to many of the best players in the world. If you watch a slow motion backswing done with this theory, you will notice that all the check-points of a perfect backswing will be achieved. The main difference is that this backswing is much simpler to learn, to perform and to repeat, requires less practice and is more reliable under pressure.

The key for a good backswing is to turn properly. Still the majority of weekend players don't understand how this rotation should be done. As the correct rotation of the shoulders is quite different from the rotation we have always been taught, the main goal of this chapter is to learn how to turn our shoulders properly.

To master the correct technique, you will need to go through the following three steps:

1. FIRST STEP: ARMS CROSSED OVER YOUR CHEST.
To understand the correct movement of the shoulders we will begin with the following drill I recommend you to do in front of a mirror.

DRILL SETUP INSTRUCTIONS

1. Stand up as if you were going to hit a ball using your usual setup position.

2. However, instead of holding a club, you want to cross your arms over your shoulders with your two forefingers touching the front of your shoulders (picture 16).

3. Feel the two points of your shoulders where your forefingers are touching, as from now on and every single time you make a backswing in the future, you must only focus on moving and rotating these two points the way I am about to teach you.

If you master the correct way to move your shoulders properly during your backswing, you will never, ever have to think or worry of your arms, hands, knees or club as they will move just fine synchronized to your shoulder rotation.

ROTATION MISCONCEPTION

For some reason I can't explain, 9 out of 10 weekend golfers will make an incorrect rotation of the shoulders when I ask them to rotate them the way they believe it should be done.

Picture 16. Setup position with hands crossed over the shoulders.

Most weekend players will incorrectly rotate their shoulders in a very shallow angle maintaining both shoulders almost parallel to the ground looking more like a baseball swing with a flat path (sequence 17).

I don't want to get too technical, but from this incorrect backswing it will be almost impossible to hit a solid and long golf shot for the following two reasons:

1. Your shoulders move in such a shallow plane that your backswing ends up being extremely flat (picture 18 - pg. 52) unless you rotated your arms during the backswing on a much higher plane which as I said before, is very difficult to master.

2. When you rotate your shoulders in such a shallow plane you will over-rotate your lower body during the backswing, losing all the coil or resistance necessary to create power (sequence 17).

You may have heard in the past that pros rotate more than 90º with their shoulders or upper body during their backswing while resisting their lower body so it doesn't rotate more than 45º. The good news is that you don't have to go to the gym to achieve this goal as rotation of less than 45º of your lower body has to do with the way you rotate your shoulders and not to how well you resist your lower body.

Sequence 17. Incorrect and flat rotation of shoulders sequence.

Picture 18. Incorrect and flat backswing as a consequence of rotating the shoulders in a shallow plane.

CORRECT SHOULDER ROTATION INSTRUCTIONS

The secret I am about to share with you will change your golf game forever. Every good golf swing has a common denominator: a correct body motion. My technique of only focusing on rotating your shoulders on the right path during the backswing will make you do a great backswing with a perfect pivot motion. The key is to spend enough time in the drill I am going to explain momentarily until you understand it and master it.

I truly recommend you practice this drill as much as you can. You can do it in front of a mirror in your house, in the elevator, in your office bathroom, etc. This drill will make you a better golfer and is much more effective than going to the practice range every day to hit hundreds of balls. So let me explain to you how to do it correctly.

STEP A – DRILL TO UNDERSTAND VERTICAL INSTEAD OF HOR-IZONTAL ROTATION CONCEPT: The key to master the correct backswing is to understand and learn how to rotate your shoulders in a steeper angle where your left shoulder is actually moving down while your right shoulder is moving up:

1.　Get back to your setup position with your arms crossed over your chest and your forefingers touching the front of your shoulders (picture 16 - pg 49).

2.　Focus on moving and rotating these two points of your shoulders during the entire backswing.

3.　Imagine you have a clock around your shoulders where the 3 o'clock position is touching your left shoulder, the 9 o'clock position is touching your right shoulder, the 6 o'clock position is under your chin and the 12 o'clock position is up and behind your neck. Please note that the watch is vertical to the ground and parallel to the target line (pictures 19 and 20 - pg 54 and 55).

Picture 19. Setup position with imaginary clock face-on.

Picture 20. Setup position with imaginary clock vertical and parallel to target line.

4. Place a club on the ground touching your shoes so it is parallel to the target line (picture 21).

Picture 21. Club parallel to target line.

5. Begin to rotate your shoulders thinking of moving your left shoulder from the 3 o'clock position to the 6 o'clock position while moving your right shoulder from the 9 o'clock position to the 12 o'clock position.

To fully understand the concept, think of rotating your shoulders parallel to the club you have on the ground (target line) in such way that your left shoulder will never cross over the club.

If you incorrectly turn your shoulders in a horizontal or shallow plane, you will see your left shoulder cross over the club on the ground giving you immediate feed-back that you have not yet been able to turn your shoulders vertically.

6. The purpose of this drill is to teach you how to rotate your shoulders vertically but please keep in mind that this will not be your exact backswing.

As a matter of fact, if you make this drill perfectly, you will notice that you are either not going to be able to take your left shoulder all the way to the 6 o'clock position (picture 22) or you will end up doing a reverse pivot (picture 23) which is also incorrect as your weight would not be transferred to your right side during the backswing.

Picture 22. Shoulder rotation parallel to target line thus not being able to take your left shoulder all the way to the 6 o'clock position.

Picture 23. Shoulder rotation parallel to target line thus making a reverse pivot.

STEP B – MAKE A PERFECT BACKSWING: Now that you learned how the shoulders should move, let me introduce a minor change to the previous drill that will make you do a perfectly solid backswing:

1. Repeat the first 3 steps of the previous drill: Setup position with arms across your chest, focus on only moving your two shoulders and think of the imaginary clock.

2. Place a club on the ground as you did before. However, this time you want the club to aim slightly to the right of the target line. To do this, make the club touch your right shoe but separate the club from the left shoe by one inch (picture 24).

 Picture 24. Club aiming to the right slightly to the inside of the target line.

3. Begin, as you did before, to rotate your shoulders thinking of moving your left shoulder from the 3 o'clock position to the 6 o'clock position while moving your right shoulder from the 9 o'clock position to the 12 o'clock position.

Think of rotating your shoulders parallel to the club you have on the ground, thus, this time you will still rotate vertically but slightly to the inside of the target line.

Although this may sound a little complicated while you read it, please give it a try. **You will find out that this time, your left shoulder will easily get to the 6 o'clock position and you will be making a perfect backswing with a perfect body rotation** (sequence 25 - pg 60).

If you were able to rotate your shoulders the way I just explained, which I am sure you did, I am proud to tell you that you have learned how to make a good backswing and are ready to take your game to the next level.

If a professional teacher had the chance to watch you doing this drill properly, he would immediately see you making a perfect pivot motion of the body with a rotation of your shoulders of at least 90° while resisting your lower body, creating the coil necessary to develop power and accuracy.

Sequence 25. Correct rotation of shoulders sequence.

From now on and on every backswing you make in the future, all you need to do is to move your shoulders the exact way you just did. Of course, you will be holding the club instead of crossing your arms around your chest.

2.   SECOND STEP: BACKSWING SIMULATION WITHOUT HOLDING A CLUB YET

Now that you understand the correct movement of the shoulders we will move on to a drill that will familiarize you with the feeling of making a backswing while only thinking of rotating your shoulders:

BACKSWING DRILL WITHOUT A CLUB

1.   Take your normal stance as if you are going to hit a golf ball (picture 26).

Picture 26. Setup position with no club.

2. Move your Upper Arms towards your body so they touch and create some pressure against the sides of your chest, as explained in the previous chapter.

3. Just as you did with the crossed arms drill, begin to rotate your shoulders thinking of moving your left shoulder from the 3 o'clock position to the 6 o'clock position while moving your right shoulder from the 9 o'clock position to the 12 o'clock position. Remember that you want to move your shoulders vertically and parallel to an imaginary line that slightly moves to the inside of the target line (picture 24 - pg 58).

CHECK-POINTS

The key to check here is to ensure that your left shoulder touches your chin by the time your left arm is parallel to the ground (picture 27). This can easily be done if you rotate the shoulders on the correct path.

While it is common to hear the experts say that at this point of the swing you should have completed about two thirds of your turn, I don't believe in that.

I invite you to watch a couple of the tour player's backswings on www.pgatour.com/swingplex and you will see for yourself that most players have turned 90° by the time their left arm is parallel to the ground. This is a good key for distance.

 Picture 27. Halfway backswing where left shoulder touches chin and left arm is parallel to the ground.

3.   THIRD AND FINAL STEP: REAL BACKSWING

Believe it or not you already know how to make a perfect backswing (sequence 28 - pg 64). You just need to trust yourself. From now on it doesn't matter if you are on the practice range or on the tee of hole number one. Just remember your setup keys (upper-arms and chest connection with hands relaxed) and you are ready to go.

Your challenge will be to forget whatever you used to think during the backswing and only think of moving your shoulders the way you have learned in the previous steps.

Sequence 28. Correct backswing sequence.

Remember that if you master the correct way to move your shoulders properly during your backswing, you will never have to think or worry of your arms, hands, knees or club as they will move just fine synchronized with your shoulder rotation.

As your arms are going to move synchronized with your shoulders, I am happy to tell you that only thinking of your shoulders while having a setup that connects your arms with your chest will ensure that you will make a one-plane swing, just as Tiger's or Steve Stricker's backswing (pictures 9 and 10 - pgs 32 and 33).

As the key to this backswing is to master the shoulder turn, I vastly recommend that instead of doing a practice swing with your club on the course, do it with your hands across your chest, just as the drill explained in step number one.

While doing this practice drill, just before you hit every shot, feel the path your shoulders are moving back. Then, when you hold the club, you will be surprised on how easy it will be to rotate your shoulders on the right track, taking advantage of your muscle memory. This is the way I play and it is part of my pre-shot routine. While doing the practice drill, I place the club I am about to hit towards my upper leg joint so it doesn't fall (picture 29 - pg 66).

Picture 29. Pre-shot shoulder rotation routine with club towards upper leg joint.

7. MY METHOD: TRANSITION KEY – CREATING LAG

As I mentioned before, one of the most important aspects to create club speed and pure ball striking common in absolutely every tour player's golf swing is "lag". Lag could be defined as the trailing of the club behind the hands during the downswing. If you ever heard of "Ben Hogan's magical move" it referred exactly to this concept. In our times, one of the most popular players known for the amount of lag created during the downswing is Sergio Garcia. This explains why he hits the ball so far even though he is so small (5 feet 10 inches tall and 160 lbs) when compared to other players. Sergio has been many times in the top ten in Driving Distance and number one in Total Driving.

Actually, the reason you not only see Sergio Garcia but every tour player developing such high clubhead speeds, many times above

125 MPH, while doing an effortless and smooth swing has to do with the amount of lag they create.

Of course, a good backswing is the foundation for having a good transition and downswing. However, a good backswing does not guarantee a good downswing. A good player may have a perfect backswing and still come over the top when coming down.

Without any doubt, being able to increase lag during the downswing is one of the major differences between the golf swing of an amateur versus a pro (picture 3 - pg 17). You see single digit handicap players that play decent golf without increasing their lag or wrist cock during the downswing as pros do. As a matter of fact, I have played golf for almost 30 years and only until a year ago was I really able to understand this concept and incorporate it in my golf swing. From that moment, I immediately started hitting the ball harder and more solidly. For perspective, I can tell you my driver carry distance automatically increased from 260 yards to 290 yards. Please keep in mind that I live more than eight thousand feet above sea level where there is less resistance in the air and the ball flies 10% more.

The big breakthrough that I made and that I will teach you shortly is that lag is not a consequence of great flexibility or any special physical ability, but has to do with the force of inertia or the resistance of the clubhead to a change in its state of motion that occurs in the transition between the backswing and the downswing. I understand this can sound complicated but the good news is that any golfer that understands the concept that I am about to explain can learn how to lag the club like the pros, increasing dramatically his clubhead speed, thus maximizing his ball striking ability and distance.

So for now just keep in mind that the more lag you can create, the longer and better you will hit the golf ball.

WHY LAG CREATES HIGHER CLUBHEAD SPEEDS: Other than wind, temperature and altitude, there are only three variables that determine how far the ball travels: ball speed, launch angle and spin rate. It is true that the best players in the world make fine adjustments to their swings and do proper club fitting to obtain optimal launch angles and spin rates for their particular ball speeds, in order to maximize their distance. Still and by far, the most important variable that determines distance is ball speed.

Ball speed is the result of multiplying clubhead speed times "smash factor" which is a ratio that measures how pure the quality of the contact was. The closer you hit the ball with the center of gravity of the club usually known as the "sweet spot", the most amount of energy will be transferred from the club to the ball and the higher the smash factor will be. Professional golfers usually have a smash factor of around 1.47. For perspective purposes, the average driver ball speed on the PGA tour is 165 mph that result from multiplying an average clubhead speed of 112 mph times a smash factor of 1.47.

In other words, in order to increase your distance you need to increase your ball speed. And in order to increase your ball speed you need to hit it solidly and to develop the maximum clubhead speed possible at the moment of impact.

The key here is to understand that even if your hands and arms may travel at the same speed during the swing, your clubhead does not. If you have the opportunity to watch a slow motion swing of a tour player, you can see that at the beginning of the downswing the clubhead is moving slowly until suddenly it starts to accelerate, generating the maximum speed right when the club reaches the ball (at impact position). This incredible acceleration is the result of the club "lagging" behind the hands for as far and for as long as possible until the club is finally released and has to speed up dramatically to be able to reach the hands, which it does right after the ball has been hit. This acceleration of the clubhead is almost impossible to perceive when you watch a player on TV, but it explains why tour players develop such phenomenal speeds and hit the ball so far while making such easy and smooth swings.

As an image is worth a thousand words, in (sequence 30) I am showing you visually how this acceleration takes place. As you can see, I divided the downswing into 8 frames where the elapsed time is pretty much the same from frame to frame. However, the point I want to show you is how little distance the clubhead travels at the beginning of the downswing compared to how much distance it has to travel just before impact. Obviously, the more distance needed for the clubhead to travel during the same amount of time that took the hands to move from one frame to another graphically shows that the speed of the clubhead increased dramatically during the downswing.

Sequence 30. Diagram showing acceleration of clubhead during downswing.

Now that you understand this concept, let me show you at last why increasing lag is the best way to have an instant and significant improvement in your distance and ball striking capabilities. Changing your arms and hands speed is not an easy task and most probably can only be done as a consequence of improving the quality of your swing. For instance, I expect you will hit the ball harder and better just by having improved your backswing as explained in the previous chapter. Still and for academic purposes, let's suppose you are not going to be able to increase your arms and hands speed during the downswing. The beauty of lag is that you can dramatically increase the clubhead speed just by increasing your lag or wrist cock during the downswing without having to swing your arms or hands harder or faster.

In (pictures 31a, 31b y 31c), I will compare the typical lag created during the beginning of the downswing at the moment when the left arm gets parallel to the ground of three types of players: an amateur that comes over the top, a tour player and Jamie Sadlowski who is the 2008 Remax Long Driver champion with a drive of 418 yards. Looking at these differences, you can start to perceive that distance is directly related to the amount of lag created during the downswing.

In (pictures 32a, 32b y 32c), I again compare the three club shaft positions, but this time I do it just before the hands reach the impact

Picture 31a. Typical clubhead position of an amateur coming over the top.

Picture 31b. Typical clubhead position of a tour player increasing lag.

Picture 31 c. Comparison of lag created by three types of players.

75

 Picture 32a. Typical clubhead position of an amateur coming over the top.

Picture 32b. Typical clubhead position of a tour player increasing lag.

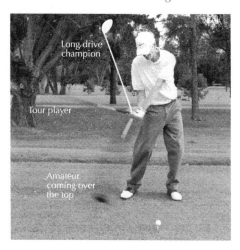

Long drive champion

Tour player

Amateur coming over the top

Picture 32c. Comparison of lag created by three types of players.

zone. Although the three players still have about the same distance for their hands to travel from this point to impact, please look at the huge difference in how much distance the clubheads of the three players still need to travel as a consequence of the amount of lag that each player was able to create. As the amateur player has created a minimum amount of lag and the clubhead is closer to the ball, he will need a clubhead speed of approximately 80 mph to catch the hands at the impact zone while the tour player's and Sadlowski's clubhead speed will have to accelerate to 112 and 150 mph respectively to release the club properly.

LAG MISCONCEPTION: A common believe tells you that you should maintain the 90 degree angle formed by the left arm and the club on the backswing during the downswing. However, when you analyze the swings of the vast majority of tour players, they increase the amount of lag during the transition of the backswing and downswing, decreasing such angle to 45 degrees or less while increasing the cocking of the wrists thus giving them higher swing speeds, distance and better ball striking (picture 31b).

The more lag you can create at the beginning of the downswing will result in a bigger lag during the entire downswing which will increase your clubhead speed at the moment of impact. The good news is that once you understand how lag is created and increased, you will notice that you can also do it, maximizing your clubhead speed for your particular swing.

HOW TO INCREASE LAG: To understand how to increase lag, we always have to remember that this phenomenon can only be done thanks to the force of inertia or the resistance of the clubhead to change its state of motion that occurs during the transition of the backswing and the downswing.

To put it in simpler words, through the backswing, the clubhead is smoothly moving back until the player suddenly starts the downswing changing the direction in which the club has been moving. As the force of inertia will try to resist this change of direction, when the transition is done properly, you will see for a fraction of a second that the grip of the club has already started to move towards the target while the clubhead is still moving back.

As a matter of fact, when you watch a tour player swing in slow motion, you can see that at some point during the transition, the lower body has already started to move towards the target while the clubhead is still moving up completing the backswing. Based on this observation, it is not unusual to hear that you should begin your downswing before you finish your backswing. Trying to do this could drive you crazy. This could be equivalent to trying to run in two directions at the same time. Again, the only reason this happens has to do with the force of inertia. Although the player has finished his backswing and has begun his downswing immediately after, the clubhead will continue to move back for a fraction of second as the clubhead doesn't want to change its direction.

On the other hand, it is not possible to increase lag during the downswing if you make a complete stop at the top of the backswing. In this hypothetical scenario, the clubhead will not try to keep moving back when you begin your downswing as it was not moving back when you changed the direction of your swing.

Although this may sound complicated, the best and easiest way to understand how this inertia force helps us increase lag is to feel it. To do this I have designed the following drills that will help you do just that. Please pay full attention, as the only way to implement more lag to your swing is to understand how it feels:

1.   FIRST LAG DRILL: PUTT WITH A HAND TOWEL.

1.   Find a hand towel, take your normal grip for a long shot but make your normal swing for a long putt. Perhaps you need to take the towel back slower in order to keep it straight.

2.   Now change direction as you normally do when you putt accelerating your stroke towards the target. Notice how the lower

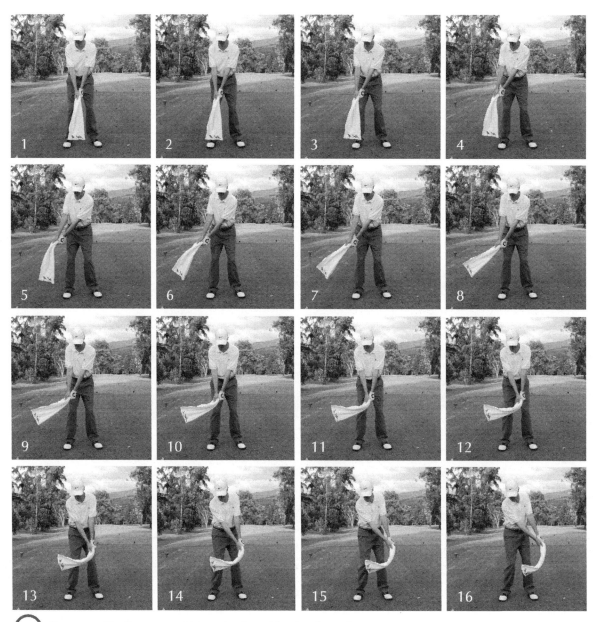

Sequence 33. Sequence of increasing lag with a hand towel.

part of the towel moves to your right when your hands started moving to your left (Sequence 33).

This situation where for a moment the upper part of the towel started moving towards the target while the lower part of the towel was moving in the opposite direction, due to the force of inertia, is exactly what we need to learn to do with the golf club.

2)   SECOND LAG DRILL: FEEL LAG WITH YOUR RIGHT HAND ONLY.

1.   Take a golf club with your right hand only. Imagine that the grip of the club is the upper part of the towel while the clubhead is the lower part of the towel.

2.   Make a long putt backswing where your wrists don't hinge very much.

3.   Now change the direction accelerating your right hand towards the target. You should feel like if you were pushing just the grip of the club towards the target in a way that your goal is to have the grip arrive to the impact zone before the clubhead does (sequence 34 - pg 82).

Sequence 34. Sequence of increasing lag with right hand only.

CHECK-POINTS DURING THE TRANSITION (Img. 9 and 10, pg 82)

1. The clubhead moves to the right when your hand and grip start moving to your left.

2. The angle formed by the club shaft and the ground changes as the grip moves closer to the ground while the clubhead moves up.

3. The butt end of the grip that was touching your hand has now separated from your hand moving to the left.

3. **THIRD LAG DRILL: FEEL LAG WITH BOTH HANDS**

1. Take your normal setup and grip. Hold the club the softest you can so that the club doesn't fall.

2. Make a short swing so that your hands don't get above your waist with the least wrist hinge possible.

3. Now change direction accelerating your hands towards the target. You should feel like if you were pushing just the grip of the club towards the target in a way that your goal is to have the grip arrive first to the impact zone and then the clubhead (sequence 35 - pg 84), exactly the same as you did in the previous drill. A good swing thought to make this lag happen is to try to accelerate

Sequence 35.
Sequence of
increasing lag with
both hands.

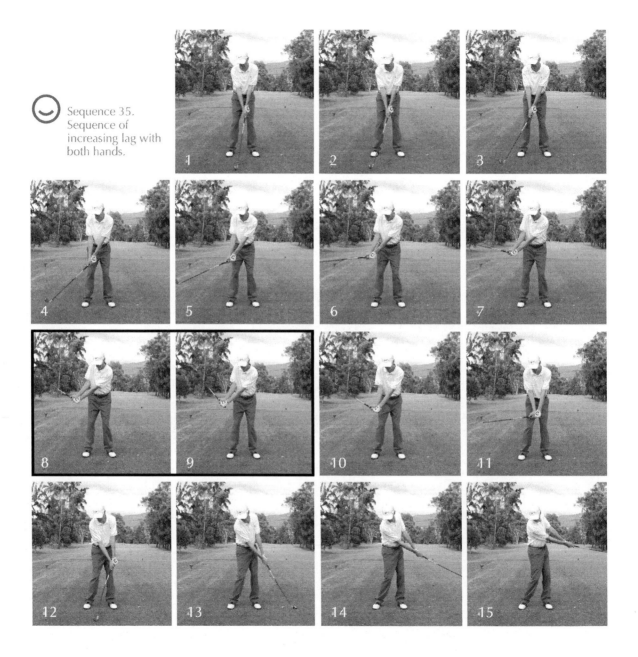

your hands and grip towards the target while trying to leave the clubhead at the top of the backswing.

CHECK-POINTS DURING THE TRANSITION (Img. 8 and 9, pg 84)

1. The clubhead moves to the right when your hands and grip start moving to your left (Same as the previous check-point).

2. The angle formed by the club shaft and the ground changes as the grip moves closer to the ground while the clubhead moves up (Same as the previous check-point).

3. Your hands and wrist cock increase. Please note this additional wrist cock is not something you try to consciously do and is only the consequence of the clubhead being pushed to the right because of the force of inertia while changing direction with the club held very softly.

The feeling of this drill should be exactly the same as the previous one when you were holding the club with the right hand. If for any reason you are not able to feel the lag increasing this time, I recommend you go back to the first two drills before moving on. Please be patient as I can guarantee that once you do it properly, you will have learned it for a lifetime.

HOW TO INCORPORATE LAG TO YOUR FULL SWING: At this point of the book I hope you are convinced of the importance of increasing lag and expect you to be anxious to incorporate it to your swing to find out how much longer and better you are able to hit the golf ball.

I also expect that by now you have a clear concept of the huge difference between coming to the ball creating lag versus coming to the ball over the top where the clubhead is launched to the ball just like if it was a fishing pole.

Technically speaking, what happens during the transition is that your weight is transferred from the right side to the left side. This weight shift begins with the lower body pulling your hands and grip towards the target while leaving the clubhead still moving to the other side.

I am a true believer that once you trigger the start of your downswing with a good transition swing thought, you should not think of anything else until you finish your swing. Moreover, once you master the technique of how to start the downswing creating lag, you may not even need to think about it anymore.

So now that you have learned how lag feels, follow these instructions to incorporate it to your real swing:

INSTRUCTIONS FOR TRANSITION WITH LAG

1. Take your normal stance making sure you connect your upper arms with your body as explained previously.

2. Remember to hold the club with your hands as soft as you can (3 on a scale from 1 to 10) with your fingers relaxed so that, hypothetically, someone could easily pull the club away from your hands.

3. Rotate your shoulders vertically and parallel to an imaginary line that slightly moves to the inside of the target line (picture 24 - pg 58).

4. Just when your backswing gets to the top, **begin your downswing thinking only of moving your right elbow towards the right side of your body** (sequence 35a – pg 88), making sure you feel the same lag sensation you felt when doing the drills. The faster you move your elbow towards your side, the bigger the lag you will create and the further the ball will go.

Although the orthodox swing thoughts during the transition are to start moving your weight from the right foot to the left foot or by sliding your hips to the left side and parallel to the target line, these don't guarantee you will increase lag.

On the other hand, **beginning the downswing thinking only of moving your right elbow towards the right side of your body** (sequence 35a), will ensure that you make a perfect weight transfer and lag increase.

Sequence 35a. Movement of the elbow towards the side of the body.

8. THREE QUARTER SWINGS AND SHORT GAME

The fundamentals I have taught you through this book (stance, backswing and transition) should be used on every full swing shot you have from the sand-wedge to the driver. You can also use them when you have a three quarter swing. For example, I hit my 56 degree sand-wedge 115 yards and often make a three quarter swing using the same principals when I need to hit the ball 100 yards. I also make a three quarter backswing when I am in a distance that gets me in between clubs or when I need the ball to fly lower and with less spin. In both of the previous examples I use the longer club and make a three quarter backswing.

Please notice that the backswing technique of rotating the shoulders should not be used on the short game. When I refer to short game, I am thinking of every shot from 50 yards in or shots where you make less than half swing. The short game requires a different technique that I will not cover in detail in this book as it was not the purpose of this project.

However, as a good short game is a must if you want to score your best, I am going to briefly explain the basic chip or pitch shot that you can use on any shot from the fringe and back to 50 yards away from the hole, including the bunker:

SHORT GAME FUNDAMENTALS

1. Take your stance with your weight slightly forward toward the target and your hands ahead of the clubhead so that your left arm forms a straight line with the club shaft before you begin your swing. As the key of the short game is to get to the impact zone with your hands ahead of the clubhead, this initial position will give you more room for error allowing you to hit the ball crisply (sequence 36).

2. Take out the club only thinking of breaking the wrists. A good backswing thought is to immediately fold the line formed by the club and your left arm with your hands. Please notice this should be the same technique used for any short shot from the fringe and back to 50 yards. The only adjustment that should be made is the length of the backswing.

3. Just as your long game, begin your downswing by only trying to leave the clubhead at the top of the backswing for as long as possible, making sure you feel the same lag sensation you felt when doing the drills.

Sequence 36. Short game pitch shot sequence.

4. Open your clubface if you want the ball to fly higher and land softer. Before you begin your swing, remember to adjust your stance so the clubface aims towards the target.

TIP: The secret of the short game in order to be able to hit crisp and consistent approaches is to create some lag. So besides starting your backswing breaking your wrists, the short game swing should feel just like the third lag drill: "Feel lag with both hands".

9. SUMMARY

I hope this book will help you become a better player from day one. I expect that you start making shots and rounds you had only dreamed of until now. I am sure my system works as I've seen the amazing results with players of all levels that have tried it. Still, my goal was to be able to write my swing concepts and learning method in a clear way so that anyone who reads my book without having me on their side would be able to understand it and implement it.

I am aware that some of the methods I provided in this book may initially sound difficult to implement. Please believe me it is much simpler than it appears. Once you try it on the practice range or on the golf course, you will be surprised with the results. The other good part of my system is that once you learn it, it will work for a life time. You won't need to change or evolve the swing thoughts I gave you in the future. You now understand what you need to do and to think to be able to hit solid, straight and long golf shots. If for any reason your swing struggles in a round of golf, please don't try to fix the faults. Just follow the checklist I will write down in a moment and make sure you are doing it right. Trust me that if you are able to check-mark the following points, your swing will immediately get back on track:

MY METHOD: SETUP

1. Connect your Upper Arms towards your body maintaining a pressure of 4 on a 1-10 scale.

2. Hold the club with your usual grip but as soft as you can (3/10) feeling your hands and fingers are totally relaxed.

MY METHOD: BACKSWING

1. Make your practice swing with your hands crossed over your chest instead of doing it with your club.

2. Think only of moving your shoulders, rotating them vertically and parallel to an imaginary line that moves slightly to the inside of the target line.

3. Remember the image of taking your left shoulder to the 6 o'clock position while taking the right shoulder to the 12 o'clock position.

MY METHOD: TRANSITION – CREATING LAG

1. Just when your backswing gets to the top, begin your downswing thinking only of moving your right elbow towards the right side of your body (sequence 35a – pg 88), making sure you feel the same lag sensation you felt when doing the drills.

10. SOCIAL RESPONSABILITY

I decided to write this book for two reasons.

Many years ago, I heard a wise man say that there is nothing more gratifying in this world than helping others. At that time, I really didn't fully understand the meaning of this phrase. Throughout the years I learned the lesson and can clearly associate the happiest days of my life with the few times when I have been able to touch other peoples' lives in a positive way.

Taking this consideration to a more superficial scenario, like golf, I have been surprised of the level of satisfaction that produces the improvement of the game for most weekend golfers. So having been lucky enough to discover and develop a break-through method that has a significant impact in the golf level of any player in a short period of time, has given me the opportunity to share it with the people I know and to enjoy the gratifying experience of seeing their immediate progress.

So having proved how positively these findings I made can have an impact on the golf life of so many people, I felt I not only had the opportunity, but the obligation to write a book and share my knowledge with anyone interested in golf.

On the other hand, according to the United Nations, there are more than 1,000 million hungry people in the world, not to mention the small percentage that has access to education or to many other needs in today's world. I believe this situation gives us all an important social responsibility. The experts in this area believe the best social responsibility models are the ones where corporations benefit while helping.

Trying to replicate this concept in a smaller case, 50% of the profits obtained from this project will be donated to charity as I believe many of the people like you would be more than happy to do a good deed for someone else and at the same time your golf will have an unprecedented improvement.

Finally, If you feel satisfied with this book, I would really appreciate if you will recommend it to a friend and also write a positive review, as your comments will be the foundation of the marketing strategy to increase the word of mouth needed to sell more books thus making this social responsibility project a relevant one.

END

Made in the USA
Lexington, KY
01 July 2011